YAB

Helps You Navigate

MIDDLE SCHOOL

You can do this!

Written by Krista Betcher

Illustrated by Kevin Cannon

Beaver's Pond Press

For CJ and Kyle, who have
shined through many life
transitions. I'm proud
to be your mom.

– Krista Betcher

For Maggie, for always
being a voice of calm
and reason. Thanks for
reminding me to breathe.

– Kevin Cannon

Edited by Hanna Kjeldbjerg
Illustrated by Kevin Cannon

ISBN 13: 978-1-59298-636-1

Library of Congress Catalog Number: 2018904428

Printed in the United States of America
First Printing: 2018

22 21 20 19 18   5 4 3 2 1

Book design and typesetting by Kevin Cannon

BEAVER'S
POND
PRESS

Beaver's Pond Press, Inc.
7108 Ohms Lane
Edina, MN 55439-2129
(952) 829-8818
www.BeaversPondPress.com

To order, visit www.ItascaBooks.com
or call (800) 901-3480. Reseller discounts available.

Contact Krista Betcher at www.KristaBetcher.com for school visits, speaking
engagements, freelance writing projects, and interviews.

Thank you to:

my students through the years; you made me a better teacher.

my MSL groups, who showed me that our world is in good hands with you as leaders.

Hanna Kjeldbjerg, for her never-ending energy and guidance.

Kevin Cannon, for bringing my vision to life with his amazing talent.

— Krista Betcher

Thank you to:

Krista Betcher, for sharing your vision with the world and letting me illustrate it!

Hanna Kjeldbjerg, for continually inspiring us with your passion for publishing.

— Kevin Cannon

I'll share another interesting fact about myself:

I live in your **BRAIN**!

I'm in your **PREFRONTAL CORTEX**—that's
the part of your brain that helps you make good decisions.

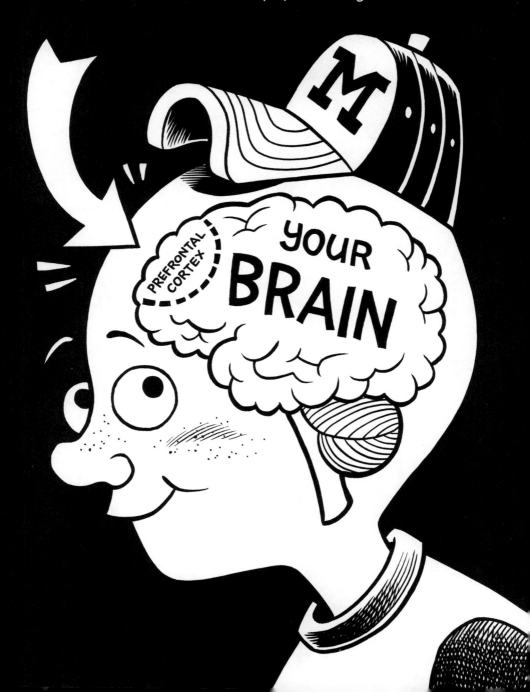

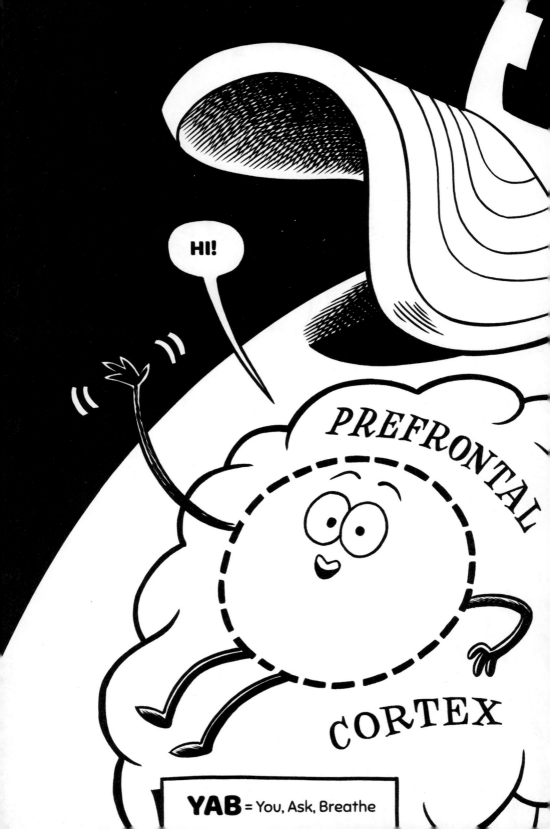

How does **YOUR** YAB look?

YAB = You, Ask, Breathe

DRAW YOUR YAB!

Now, I'm going to share some tips that will help your transition to middle school!

YAB = You, Ask, Breathe

How are the
TEACHERS
at the middle school?

Will they be compassionate?

Will they be strict?

YAB = You, Ask, Breathe

What's the
HOMEWORK load?

How much homework will I have?

Will the homework be difficult?

YAB = You, Ask, Breathe

Will I have
FRIENDS?

Will my current friends stay the same?

Will I make new friends?

YAB = You, Ask, Breathe

Will I have a
LOCKER?

Are lockers hard to open?

Will I ever learn to open my locker?

YAB = You, Ask, Breathe

YAB = You, Ask, Breathe

Your brain must be boggled with so many questions.

That's where I come in!

I have a few tips to help you navigate this big change.

YAB = You, Ask, Breathe

As a new middle schooler, keep these things in mind:

YOU,
ASK,
BREATHE.

First, be yourself!

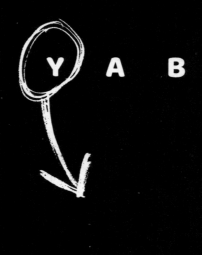

YOU

YAB = You, Ask, Breathe

Who are you?

What's important to you?

What do you value?

What makes your heart smile?

What are your hobbies?

What do you like to do in your free time?

Next, ask questions.

ASK

YAB = You, Ask, Breathe

There are many people who will help you!

Teachers will help you get settled into your new routine.

Do you have siblings or friends who are already at the middle school? They will be able to answer your questions ... you just have to ask!

Any adult in the building is able to help.

Older students are able to help.

Last, take a breath.

Y A B

BREATHE

YAB = You, Ask, Breathe

Stop, pause, and take a breath.

Think about shaking a glitter jar or a snow globe.

You know how the glitter settles on the bottom after you shake it?

The glitter or snow is like your brain when it's boggled.

Your brain needs a moment to settle.

It's the same way the snow settles on the bottom of a
snow globe after it's been shaken.

There's no doubt that going to middle school is a big change in your life.

YAB = You, Ask, Breathe

ACTIVITY SECTION

Let's put **YAB** into action!

YOU

YAB = You, Ask, Breathe

 Write your name and design the space.

 Color the heart. In the puzzle pieces behind the heart, write and/or draw people, places, or things that make your heart smile!

 How do you help others?

 Write words in the spaces to show what makes you unique and one of a kind!

 What grounds you and gives you roots?

 How do you learn best? Do you enjoy reading to learn, listening to learn, creating to learn, or a combination of any of those?

ASK

My question

People who can answer this question

My question

People who can answer this question

YAB = You, Ask, Breathe

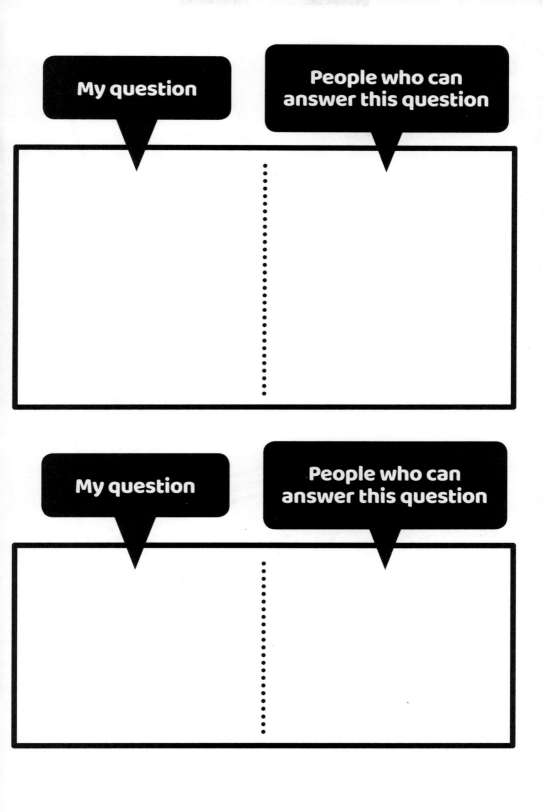

1 Place yourself in a comfy, cozy position. Close your eyes if that will help you focus **OR** choose something to focus on within the room. It could be a spot on the wall or the floor.

2 Hold out your hand.

3 With one finger of your other hand, gently trace around each of your fingers. As you trace up to the tip of your finger, inhale. As you trace back down, exhale.

EXHALE

INHALE

4 Focus your thoughts on your breath. Where do you feel your breathing? Do you feel it in your stomach? Do you feel it in your nose?

5 Now, count as you trace each finger. While tracing your thumb, inhale up the thumb and exhale down the other side while counting ONE. Move on to the second finger. Inhale up, exhale down, and count TWO. Continue this pattern with all of your fingers and you will count to FIVE.

TWO
THREE
FOUR
FIVE
ONE

6 When you're finished, allow yourself to slowly open your eyes or shift the focus of your eyes.

open

Congratulations!

You've given your brain a few moments to calm down—just like the glitter jar or snow globe settles to the bottom.

Student Advice

These pages are for you to write or draw ANYTHING! Write more questions you have about middle school! Draw another YAB! Create something that's one of a kind! Have fun!

YAB = You, Ask, Breathe

YAB = You, Ask, Breathe

About the Author

Krista Betcher is a mom, a teacher, and a creator. Throughout her career, Krista taught various grades and found her passion in the middle school "transition" years. It is her hope that students will remember the bits of advice offered by *YAB* as they venture into a new chapter in their lives.

About the Illustrator

Kevin Cannon has spent his career illustrating children's books and graphic novels, as well as writing for comic books like *SpongeBob* and *Adventure Time*. His love of drawing developed in middle school, where he wrote and illustrated tons of short stories. He lives in Minnesota with his wonderful wife, Maggie.

For more information about *YAB*, visit www.KristaBetcher.com